PLASTIC
Baskets for the Door™

By Lee Lindeman

General Instructions

Size: 7½ inches W x 9¾ inches H
(19cm x 24.8cm) without embellishments
Skill Level: Beginner

Materials

- Clear 7-count plastic canvas
- Uniek Needloft plastic canvas yarn as listed in color key for individual project
- Sewing thread in color listed for individual project
- Felt in color listed for individual project
- Sawtooth hanger
- Needles: #16 tapestry, sewing needle

Stitching Step by Step

1 Cut basket front and basket back from plastic canvas according to graphs. *Note: These graphs are used for all designs in this book* except *the Summer Basket, page 17, which has its own graph for the basket front.*

2 Using the plastic canvas pieces as templates, cut matching pieces from felt in the color specified for the individual design. Trim the felt slightly smaller all around so that it will not obscure the outermost row of holes in the plastic canvas pieces.

3 Using the yarn color specified for the individual design and referring to the Scotch Stitch diagram on page 4, stitch the basket front and back according to graphs.

4 Using sewing needle and matching thread, stitch the felt to the wrong side of both stitched basket pieces.

5 Lay basket front felt side down on right side of basket back with edges even. Using matching yarn, Whipstitch basket pieces together along matching edges. Overcast remaining edges. *Note: For Valentine's Day Basket only, work Whipstitching and Overcasting in a contrasting color as specified in those instructions.*

6 Using sewing needle and thread, stitch a sawtooth hanger to wrong side of basket handle.

7 Complete assembly as described for individual design.

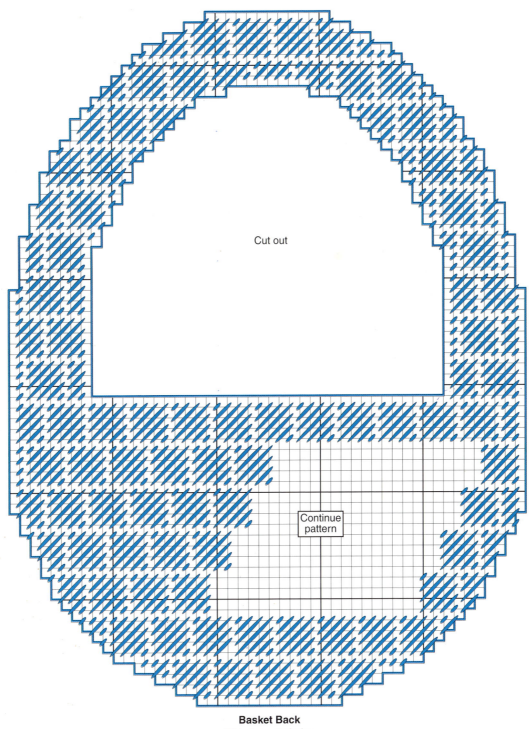

Basket Back
50 holes x 65 holes
Cut 1 for each basket

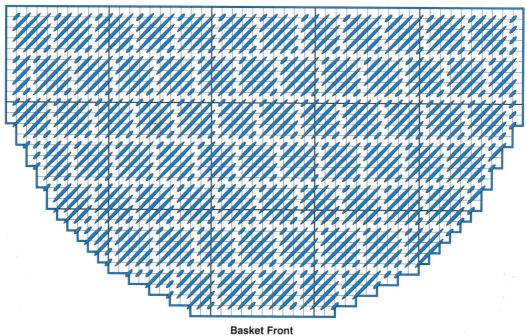

Basket Front
50 holes x 29 holes
Cut 1 for each basket

COLOR KEY	
Yards	**Plastic Canvas Yarn**
92 (84.1m)	■ Color given in individual instructions

Scotch Stitch

Winter Basket

Size: 10 inches W x 11¼ inches H
(25.4cm x 28.6cm)
Skill Level: Beginner

Materials

- 2 artist-size sheets clear 7-count plastic canvas
- Uniek Needloft plastic canvas yarn as listed in color key
- Tapestry thread as listed in color key
- 2 (6mm) black half-ball eyes
- 2 (3/8-inch/0.9cm) black half-ball buttons
- 3/8-inch (0.9cm) crystal star-shaped cabochon or sequin
- 17 (¼-inch/7mm) white pompoms
- Orange oven-bake clay
- 4 (3-inch/10.2cm) twigs
- 1-inch (2.5cm) imitation evergreen sprig
- Red satin ribbon:
    9 inches (22.9cm) 3/8-inch/9mm-wide
    6 inches (15.2cm) ⅛-inch/3mm-wide
- Royal blue sewing thread
- Felt: royal blue; red and black (optional)
- Faux suede fabric (optional): red, black
- Fiberfill
- Sawtooth hanger
- Needles: #16 tapestry, sewing needle
- Hot-glue gun

Stitching Step by Step

Basket

Referring to General Instructions, page 2, cut basket front and back from plastic canvas; stitch in pattern using royal yarn. Back with royal blue felt. Sew sawtooth hanger to reverse side of basket handle at center top.

Snowman

1 Cut two snowman pieces from plastic canvas according to graph.

2 Stitch snowman pieces according to graph, filling in uncoded area with white Continental Stitches.

3 When background stitching is complete, use 2 strands black tapestry thread to Straight Stitch mouth on one snowman.

4 Using matching colors of yarn, Whipstitch snowman pieces together, wrong sides facing, tucking in a little fiberfill before closing and sandwiching ends of twig arms between halves of snowman where indicated by arrows.

5 Following manufacturer's instructions, form a ½-inch carrot-shaped nose with a flat base from orange oven-bake clay; let cool.

6 Referring to photo throughout, glue nose to snowman; glue on 6mm half-ball eyes. Glue half-ball buttons to snowman's body.

7 Referring to pattern, cut four mittens from red felt or faux suede. Glue two mittens over end of each twig arm, sandwiching twig between layers.

8 Referring to pattern, cut one hat brim from black felt or faux suede. Fit over snowman head; glue to head at base of black stitching. Wrap ⅛-inch (3mm) ribbon around hat at brim; glue ends on back. Glue evergreen sprig over ribbon as shown.

9 Tie 3/8-inch (9mm) ribbon around neck for scarf.

Trees

1 Cut large tree and small tree from plastic canvas according to graphs.

2 Stitch trees and Overcast edges using white and holly yarns according to graphs.

3 Glue short pieces of twigs to reverse side of trees for trunks.

Assembly

1 Referring to photo throughout, glue trees to basket front. Glue pompoms in place.

2 Glue star sequin to upper right area of handle.

3 Tuck snowman into basket; secure with glue or stitches as desired.

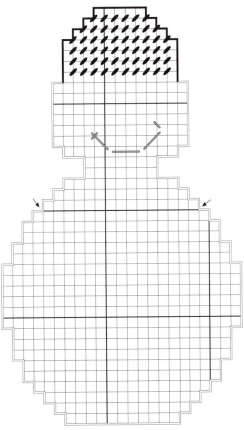

Snowman
23 holes x 39 holes
Cut 2

Mitten
Cut 4 from red felt

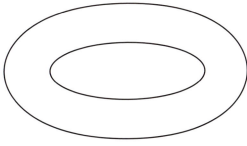

Hat Brim
Cut 1 from black felt

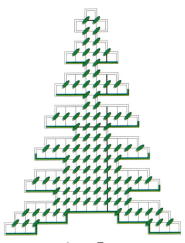

Large Tree
17 holes x 21 holes
Cut 1

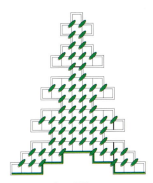

Small Tree
13 holes x 15 holes
Cut 1

COLOR KEY

Yards	Plastic Canvas Yarn
3 (2.7m)	■ Black #00
5 (4.6m)	■ Holly #27
92 (84.1m)	■ Royal #32
23 (21m)	Uncoded areas are white #41 Continental Stitches
	╱ White #41 Overcast and Whipstitch
Tapestry Thread	
5 (4.6m)	╱ Black (2-strand) Straight Stitch

Color numbers given are for Uniek Needloft plastic canvas yarn.

The Needlecraft Shop • Berne, IN 46711 • DRGnetwork.com • **Baskets for the Door** 7

Valentine's Day Basket

Size: 7½ inches W x 9¾ inches H
(19cm x 24.8cm), excluding bow
Skill Level: Beginner

Materials

- 1 artist-size sheet clear 7-count plastic canvas
- Uniek Needloft plastic canvas yarn as listed in color key
- 13 (⅝-inch/15mm) embroidered rosebud clusters
- 2 yards (1.8m) ¼-inch/7mm-wide sheer pink ribbon
- Pink sewing thread
- Pink felt
- Sawtooth hanger
- 4–6 (4 x 6-inch/10.2cm x 3.2cm) note cards with envelopes
- Needles: #16 tapestry, sewing needle
- Hot-glue gun

Stitching Step by Step

Basket

Referring to General Instructions, page 2, cut basket front and back from plastic canvas. Stitch in pattern using red yarn, but Overcast and Whipstitch using pink. Back with pink felt. Sew sawtooth hanger to reverse side of basket handle at center top.

Heart

1 Cut one heart and two half-hearts from plastic canvas according to graphs.

2 Fill hearts and half-hearts with pink Continental Stitches, reversing one half-heart before stitching.

3 Lay half-hearts on top of heart with wrong side of half-hearts on right side of heart. Whipstitch hearts together along edges between arrows. Overcast remaining edges.

4 Thread a 12-inch (30.5cm) piece of ribbon through edges of half-hearts where indicated by dot on graph; tie ends in a bow on front of heart.

Assembly

1 Referring to photo throughout, glue heart to front of basket near top edge.

2 Arrange and glue 12 embroidered rosebud clusters to front of basket.

3 Fold two 9-inch (22.9cm) pieces of ribbon into a simple 3½-inch (8.9cm) bow shape. Stitch through center of bows to attach them to top of basket handle. Glue remaining rosebud cluster over center of bow.

4 Wrap remaining ribbon around a packet of note cards with envelopes; tie ribbon ends in a bow. Tuck note cards into basket.

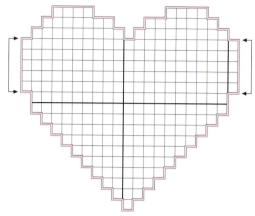

Heart
21 holes x 19 holes
Cut 1

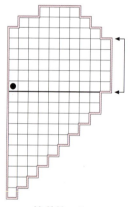

Half-Heart
10 holes x 18 holes
Cut 2, reverse 1

COLOR KEY	
Yards	**Plastic Canvas Yarn**
90 (82.3m)	■ Red #01
15 (13.7m)	Uncoded areas are pink #07 Continental Stitches
	╱ Pink #07 Overcast and Whipstitch
Color numbers given are for Uniek Needloft plastic canvas yarn.	

Spring Basket

Size: 9¼ inches W x 10 inches H
(23.5cm x 25.4cm), excluding bow
Skill Level: Beginner

Materials

- 2 artist-size sheets clear 7-count plastic canvas
- Uniek Needloft plastic canvas yarn as listed in color key
- Green plastic-coated craft wire
- 3 (⅛-inch/3mm) round purple rhinestones
- ½-inch (12mm) ladybug
- 1 yard (0.9m) 1⁷⁄₁₆-inch/38mm-wide sheer yellow wire-edge ribbon
- Pink sewing thread
- Felt: pink, yellow
- Sawtooth hanger
- Needles: #16 tapestry, sewing needle
- Hot-glue gun

Stitching Step by Step

Basket

Referring to General Instructions, page 2, cut basket front and back from plastic canvas; stitch in pattern using pink yarn. Back with pink felt. Sew sawtooth hanger to reverse side of basket handle at center top.

Pansies & Leaves

1 Cut one large, six medium and eight small petals, and 15 leaves from plastic canvas according to graphs.

2 Stitch petals according to graphs, Overcasting edges with bright purple.

3 Stitch leaves according to graphs, working Backstitch at tip of leaves last, and Overcasting edges with fern.

Assembly

1 Cut three ½-inch (1.3cm) hearts from yellow felt for pansy centers.

2 *Referring to photo throughout, arrange five petals to form a small pansy:* Arrange four small petals for sides and top of flower, overlapping edges. Add medium petal at bottom. Repeat to form a second small pansy.

3 Using large and remaining medium petals, repeat step 2 to form large pansy, positioning large petal at bottom.

4 Glue a felt heart in the center of each pansy; glue a rhinestone in the center of each heart.

5 Cut three 3-inch (7.6cm) pieces of wire; bend into stem shapes. Glue two or three leaves to stems as shown.

6 Arrange pansies, stems with leaves and remaining leaves on basket as shown in photo, positioning larger pansy in center, toward top. Allow edges of pansies, stems and leaves to extend past edges of basket as shown. Glue pansies, stems and leaves in place.

7 Glue ladybug to leaf.

8 Tie ribbon in a bow around basket handle; trim ends of streamers.

Medium Petal
8 holes x 8 holes
Cut 6

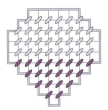

Large Petal
9 holes x 9 holes
Cut 1

Small Petal
7 holes x 8 holes
Cut 8

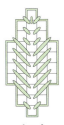

Leaf
5 holes x 10 holes
Cut 15

COLOR KEY	
Yards	**Plastic Canvas Yarn**
92 (84.1m)	■ Pink #07
11 (10.1m)	□ Fern #23
4 (3.6m)	■ Purple #46
8 (7.3m)	□ Bright purple #64
	╱ Fern #23 Backstitch
Color numbers given are for Uniek Needloft plastic canvas yarn.	

Easter Basket

Size: 7½ inches W x 9⅞ inches H
(19cm x 25.1cm)
Skill Level: Beginner

Materials
- 2 artist-size sheets clear 7-count plastic canvas
- Uniek Needloft plastic canvas yarn as listed in color key
- Tapestry thread as listed in color key
- Buttons: ½-inch (12mm) black half-round, 2 (⅝-inch/15mm) white hearts
- 2 glass eyes
- Light blue sewing thread
- Light blue felt
- Fiberfill
- 6 inches (15.2cm) ¾-inch/21mm-wide white lace
- Sawtooth hanger
- Needles: #16 tapestry, sewing needle
- Hot-glue gun

Stitching Step by Step

Basket
Referring to General Instructions, page 2, cut basket front and back from plastic canvas; stitch in pattern using bright blue yarn. Back with light blue felt. Sew sawtooth hanger to reverse side of basket handle at center top.

Bunny & Carrots

1 Cut two bunny heads, two bunny bodies, four bunny arms and three carrots from plastic canvas according to graphs.

2 Stitch one bunny head according to graph, filling in uncoded areas with white Continental Stitches. Stitch second bunny head with all white Continental Stitches.

3 Stitch remaining bunny pieces according to graphs, filling in uncoded areas with white Continental Stitches, and reversing two arms before you stitch.

4 Stitch carrots according to graph, Overcasting edges with pumpkin as you stitch.

5 When background stitching is complete, Backstitch and Straight Stitch mouth using 2 strands black tapestry thread; Straight Stitch whiskers using 2 plies brown.

Assembly

1 Using adjacent colors of yarn throughout, Whipstitch arms together in pairs, wrong sides facing, inserting a little fiberfill in each before closing.

2 Whipstitch body pieces together, wrong sides facing, inserting fiberfill before closing.

3 Overcast bottoms of both head pieces between arrows. Whipstitch heads together along remaining edges, wrong sides facing, inserting fiberfill.

4 Referring to photo throughout, place opening in bottom of head over top of body; glue in place. Glue arms to front of body as shown; glue lace around neck.

5 Glue eyes and black half-round button for nose to bunny's face. Thread pumpkin yarn through heart buttons; glue buttons to body front.

6 *Hair:* Take several stitches through top edge of head using white yarn and leaving ½-inch (1.3cm) yarn tails; frizz yarn with end of needle.

7 *Carrots:* Center and glue carrots to basket front ½ inch (1.3cm) from bottom edge. For each carrot, cut three 4-inch (10.2cm) pieces of Christmas green yarn. Hold pieces together and fold in half; wrap with another piece of Christmas green yarn ¼–½ inch (0.6–1.3cm) from fold. Trim ends even. Glue knot to basket at top of each carrot as shown in photo.

8 Tuck bunny into basket; secure with glue or stitches as desired.

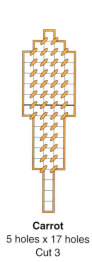

Carrot
5 holes x 17 holes
Cut 3

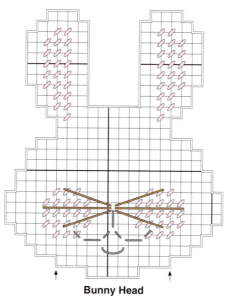

Bunny Head
21 holes x 25 holes
Cut 2
Stitch 1 as shown, stitch 1 using only white Continental Stitches

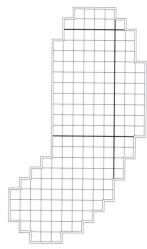

Bunny Arm
13 holes x 22 holes
Cut 4, reverse 2 before stitching

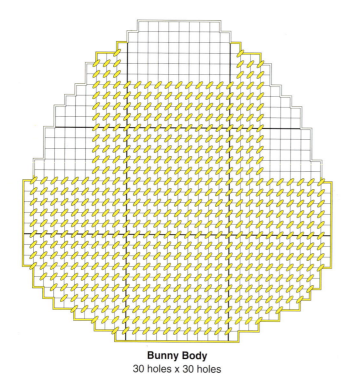

Bunny Body
30 holes x 30 holes
Cut 2

COLOR KEY

Yards	Plastic Canvas Yarn
4 (3.7m)	Pink #07
5 (4.6m)	Pumpkin #12
2 (1.8m)	Christmas green #28
34 (31.1m)	Yellow #57
92 (84.1m)	Bright blue #60
26 (23.8m)	Uncoded areas are white #41 Continental Stitches
	White #41 Overcast and Whipstitch
Tapestry Thread	
2 (1.8m)	Black (2-strand) Backstitch and Straight Stitch
1 (0.9m)	Brown (2-ply) Straight Stitch

Color numbers given are for Uniek Needloft plastic canvas yarn.

Summer Basket

Size: 7½ inches W x 9¾ inches H
(19cm x 24.8cm), excluding streamers
Skill Level: Beginner

Materials

- 1 artist-size sheet clear 7-count plastic canvas
- Uniek Needloft plastic canvas yarn as listed in color key
- 2 round wooden toothpicks
- E beads: opaque red, opaque white
- 7/16-inch (10.5mm) round wooden bead, split in half lengthwise, or 2 (7/16-inch/10.5mm) half-dome buttons
- ¾-inch (21mm) starfish
- 6 (¾- to 1½-inch/21–39mm) seashells
- 1½ yards (1.4m) ⅜-inch-wide (9mm) white satin ribbon
- Craft foam: white, red-and-white check
- Craft paints: peach, dark pink
- Black fine-tip pen
- White sewing thread
- White felt
- Sawtooth hanger
- Small paintbrush
- Needles: #16 tapestry, sewing needle
- Hot-glue gun

Stitching Step by Step

Basket

1 Referring to General Instructions, page 2, throughout, cut basket front and back from plastic canvas.

2 Stitch *back only* in pattern using bright blue yarn. Stitch front according to graph included with other graphs for this project.

3 Assemble according to General Instructions, matching colors on basket front when Whipstitching front to back.

4 Back basket with white felt. Sew sawtooth hanger to reverse side of basket handle at center top.

Summer Scene

1 Cut sail, boat, umbrella, cloud and sun according to graphs.

2 Stitch plastic canvas pieces according to graphs, filling in uncoded areas with white Continental Stitches, and Overcasting cloud, sun and sail with matching colors as you stitch.

3 Overcast umbrella and boat with red and white yarns according to graphs.

4 *Faces:* Paint half-beads (or buttons) peach; let dry. Referring to face detail drawing, add dark pink cheeks; dot on eyes with black fine-tip pen.

Assembly

1 Referring to patterns provided on page 20, cut pennant from red-and-white check craft foam, and six seagulls from white craft foam.

2 Referring to photo throughout, glue cloud and sun to upper right section of handle; glue three seagulls to handle as shown.

3 *Sailboat:* Glue toothpick to reverse side of sail along long straight edge, leaving ½ inch (1.3cm) protruding from top. Glue straight end of pennant to toothpick as shown; glue red E bead to top of toothpick.

4 Glue boat and sail to basket front, positioning bottom of toothpick mast behind boat where indicated by blue line on boat graph. Glue faces to top edge of boat as shown.

5 *Beach umbrella:* Glue white E bead to tip of toothpick; glue toothpick to wrong side of umbrella with bead at top. Glue umbrella and pole to basket front at an angle as shown.

6 Glue starfish to basket near bottom edge; glue remaining seagulls to basket front between umbrella and boat as shown.

7 *Streamers:* Cut ribbon into three 18-inch pieces. Holding ribbons together, fold in half; stitch folded ends to reverse side of basket, at center of bottom edge. Trim some of the ribbon ends so some streamers are not exactly the same length. Glue a seashell to the end of each streamer.

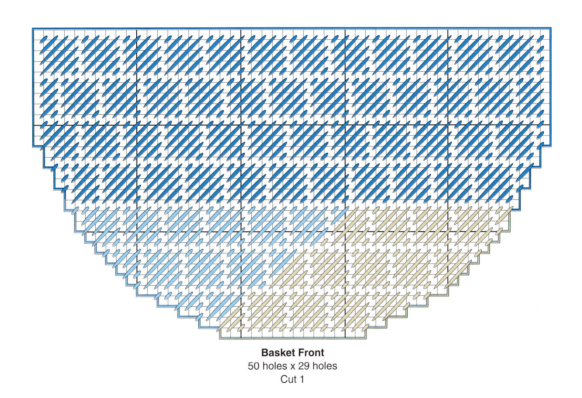

Basket Front
50 holes x 29 holes
Cut 1

COLOR KEY

Yards	Plastic Canvas Yarn
1 (0.9m)	■ Christmas red #02
7 (6.4m)	■ Sandstone #16
5 (4.6m)	■ Royal #32
1 (0.9m)	■ Yellow #57
85 (77.7m)	■ Bright blue #60
4 (3.6m)	Uncoded areas are white #41 Continental Stitches
	╱ White #41 Overcast

Color numbers given are for Uniek Needloft plastic canvas yarn.

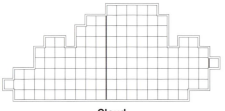

Cloud
21 holes x 9 holes
Cut 1

Boat
12 holes x 3 holes
Cut 1

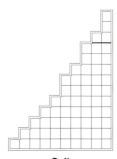

Sail
10 holes x 13 holes
Cut 1

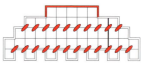

Umbrella
13 holes x 5 holes
Cut 1

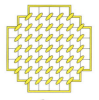

Sun
8 holes x 8 holes
Cut 1

Face Detail

Seagull
Cut 6 from white
craft foam

COLOR KEY

Yards	Plastic Canvas Yarn
1 (0.9m)	■ Christmas red #02
7 (6.4m)	■ Sandstone #16
5 (4.6m)	■ Royal #32
1 (0.9m)	■ Yellow #57
85 (77.7m)	■ Bright blue #60
4 (3.6m)	Uncoded areas are white #41 Continental Stitches
	╱ White #41 Overcast

Color numbers given are for Uniek Needloft plastic canvas yarn.

Pennant
Cut 1 from red-and-white
check craft foam

Halloween Basket

Size: 10 inches W x 11¼ inches H
(25.4cm x 28.6cm)
Skill Level: Beginner

Materials

- 2 artist-size sheets clear 7-count plastic canvas
- Uniek Needloft plastic canvas yarn as listed in color key
- Tapestry thread as listed in color key
- 4 (5mm) black half-balls
- 3 acorns
- 3-inch (7.6cm) twig
- 8 inches (20.3cm) ¼-inch/7mm-wide green satin ribbon
- Yellow sewing thread
- Yellow felt
- Sawtooth hanger
- Needles: #16 tapestry, sewing needle
- Hot-glue gun

Stitching Step by Step

Basket

Referring to General Instructions, page 2, cut basket front and back from plastic canvas; stitch in pattern using yellow yarn. Back with yellow felt. Sew sawtooth hanger to reverse side of basket handle at center top.

Ghost & Jack-o'-Lantern

1. Cut ghost and jack-o'-lantern from plastic canvas according to graphs.

2. Fill in uncoded ghost with white Continental Stitches; Overcast with black yarn. Stitch jack-o'-lantern according to graph, Overcasting with matching colors.

3. When background stitching is complete, use 2 strands black tapestry thread to Backstitch and Straight Stitch jack-o'-lantern's mouth, ghost and jack-o'-lantern's noses and chins, and to add a French knot to end of ghost's nose. To make ghost's mouth, bring up a length of thread from one end and insert needle back into other end, leaving enough slack on top to make a smile; use a small amount of glue to keep "smile" in place. Using 2 plies brown tapestry thread, work French Knot freckles on ghost.

4. Glue 5mm half-balls to ghost and jack-o'-lantern for eyes where indicated by red dots.

Leaves

1. Cut three large leaves and three small leaves from plastic canvas according to graphs.

2. Stitch two large leaves according to graph; stitch a third substituting red for brown yarn.

3. Stitch one small leaf according to graph; stitch another substituting tangerine yarn for red and the third substituting maple yarn for red.

4. Overcast edges of leaves with black yarn.

5. When background stitching is complete, use 2 strands black tapestry thread to Straight Stitch veins on leaves.

Assembly

1. Referring to photo throughout, arrange leaves on basket front, positioning large brown, small maple and small red leaves on left side and remaining leaves on right side. Glue in place.

2. Glue acorns to basket front.

3. Glue jack-o'-lantern to one end of twig; glue twig to ghost's right hand. Tie ribbon in bow around twig at bottom of jack-o'-lantern.

4. Tuck ghost into basket; secure bottom edge, head and right hand of ghost to basket with glue or stitches as desired.

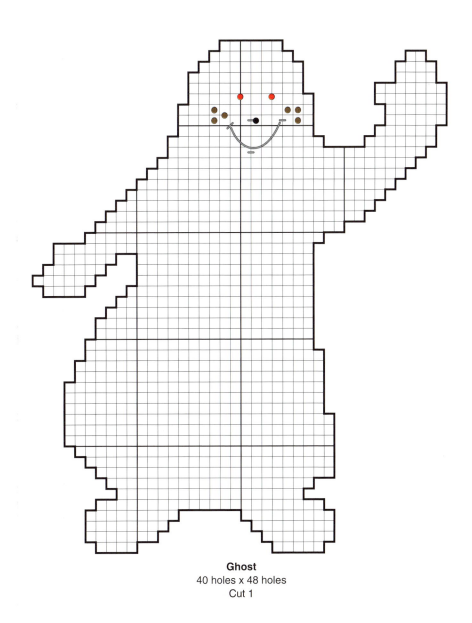

Ghost
40 holes x 48 holes
Cut 1

COLOR KEY	
Yards	**Plastic Canvas Yarn**
11 (10.1m)	■ Red #01
4 (3.7m)	Tangerine #11
3 (2.7m)	□ Pumpkin #12
5 (4.6m)	Maple #13
12 (11m)	■ Brown #15
1 (0.9m)	■ Holly #27
92 (84.1m)	■ Yellow #57
23 (21m)	Uncoded areas are white #41 Continental Stitches
6 (5.5m)	╱ Black #00 Overcast
	Tapestry Thread
5 (4.6m)	╱ Black (2-strand) Backstitch and Straight Stitch
	● Black (2-strand) French Knot
1 (0.9m)	● Brown (2-ply) French Knot
	● Attach 5mm half-ball
Color numbers given are for Uniek Needloft plastic canvas yarn.	

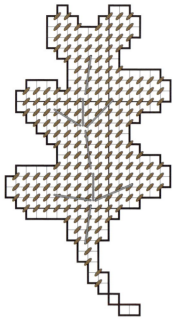

Large Leaf
16 holes x 29 holes
Cut 3
Stitch 2 as shown
Stitch 1 substituting red for brown

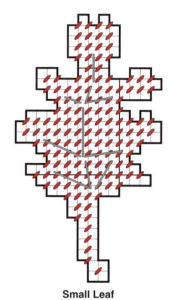

Small Leaf
14 holes x 25 holes
Cut 3
Stitch 1 as shown
Stitch 1 substituting tangerine for red
Stitch 1 substituting maple for red

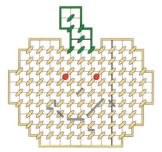

Jack-o'-Lantern
14 holes x 13 holes
Cut 1

COLOR KEY	
Yards	**Plastic Canvas Yarn**
11 (10.1m)	■ Red #01
4 (3.7m)	Tangerine #11
3 (2.7m)	Pumpkin #12
5 (4.6m)	Maple #13
12 (11m)	Brown #15
1 (0.9m)	Holly #27
92 (84.1m)	Yellow #57
23 (21m)	Uncoded areas are white #41 Continental Stitches
6 (5.5m)	╱ Black #00 Overcast
	Tapestry Thread
5 (4.6m)	╱ Black (2-strand) Backstitch and Straight Stitch
	● Black (2-strand) French Knot
1 (0.9m)	● Brown (2-ply) French Knot
	● Attach 5mm half-ball
Color numbers given are for Uniek Needloft plastic canvas yarn.	

Thanksgiving Basket

Size: 7½ inches W x 11 inches H (19cm x 27.9cm), excluding wheat
Skill Level: Beginner

Materials

- ❑ 2 artist-size sheets clear 7-count plastic canvas
- ❑ Uniek Needloft plastic canvas yarn as listed in color key
- ❑ 2 (⅜-inch/9mm) wiggly eyes
- ❑ Ornamental wheat
- ❑ 1 yard (0.9m) 1⅝-inch/39mm-wide olive green ribbon
- ❑ Peach sewing thread
- ❑ Peach felt
- ❑ Black craft foam
- ❑ Fiberfill
- ❑ Sawtooth hanger
- ❑ Needles: #16 tapestry, sewing needle
- ❑ Hot-glue gun

Stitching Step by Step

Basket

Referring to General Instructions, page 2, cut basket front and back from plastic canvas; stitch in pattern using pale peach yarn. Back with peach felt. Sew sawtooth hanger to reverse side of basket handle at center top.

Turkey

1 Cut tail feathers, two feet, two wings, two heads and two bodies according to graphs.

2 Stitch plastic canvas according to graphs. Overcast tail feathers and wings using black yarn.

3 Fold a 9-inch piece of red yarn in half; twist doubled yarn, holding ends, until yarn doubles back on itself. Without releasing twists, thread ends of yarn through one stitched turkey head where indicated by blue dot on graph; secure on reverse side, leaving 1-inch (2.5cm) wattle dangling down turkey's face.

4 Using black yarn throughout, Whipstitch head, feet and body pieces together in matching pairs, wrong sides facing, and stuffing head and body with a little fiberfill before closing completely.

5 Referring to pattern on page 28, cut two turkey beaks from black craft foam; glue together. Referring to photo throughout, glue back edge to head just below wattle so that wattle hangs down right side of beak.

6 Glue eyes to turkey as shown.

7 Glue head and wings to body. Glue body to tail feathers with bottom edges even. Glue body and tail feathers to feet, aligning bottom edge of tail feathers with blue line on feet graph.

Leaves

1 Cut two leaves from plastic canvas according to graph.

2 Stitch leaves according to graph; Overcast edges using black yarn.

Assembly

1 Referring to photo throughout, glue side edges of turkey's tail feathers and back edges of feet to basket front.

2 Arrange leaves on basket handle; glue in place. Tie ribbon in a 3¾-inch (9.5cm) bow; glue to handle over ends of leaves.

3 Tuck wheat into basket; secure with glue as desired.

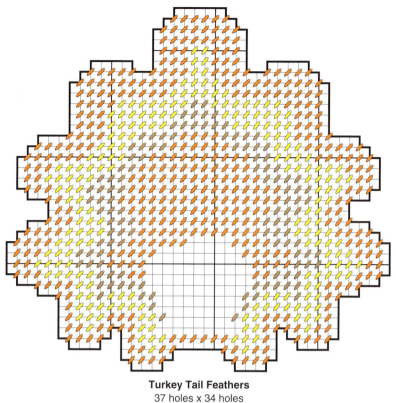

Turkey Tail Feathers
37 holes x 34 holes
Cut 1

COLOR KEY

Yards	Plastic Canvas Yarn
4 (3.7m)	■ Black #00
3 (2.7m)	■ Red #01
5 (4.6m)	■ Pumpkin #12
4 (3.7m)	■ Maple #13
10 (9.1m)	■ Brown #15
92 (84.1m)	■ Pale peach #56
6 (5.5m)	■ Yellow #57
	○ Attach wattle

Color numbers given are for Uniek Needloft plastic canvas yarn.

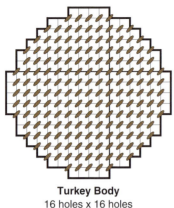

Turkey Body
16 holes x 16 holes
Cut 2

Thanksgiving Leaf
17 holes x 17 holes
Cut 2

Turkey Wing
6 holes x 6 holes
Cut 2

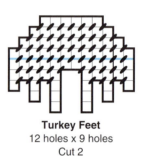

Turkey Feet
12 holes x 9 holes
Cut 2

Turkey Beak
Cut 2 from black craft foam

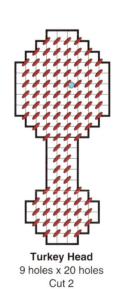

Turkey Head
9 holes x 20 holes
Cut 2

COLOR KEY

Yards	Plastic Canvas Yarn
4 (3.7m)	■ Black #00
3 (2.7m)	■ Red #01
5 (4.6m)	■ Pumpkin #12
4 (3.7m)	■ Maple #13
10 (9.1m)	■ Brown #15
92 (84.1m)	■ Pale peach #56
6 (5.5m)	■ Yellow #57
	○ Attach wattle

Color numbers given are for Uniek Needloft plastic canvas yarn.

28 Baskets for the Door • The Needlecraft Shop • Berne, IN 46711 • DRGnetwork.com

Christmas Holiday Basket

Size: 10½ inches W x 10¾ inches H (26.7cm x 27.3cm), excluding streamers
Skill Level: Beginner

Materials

- 2 artist-size sheets clear 7-count plastic canvas
- Uniek Needloft plastic canvas yarn as listed in color key
- Craft cord as listed in color key
- 12 (5mm) round gold beads
- Yellow craft foam
- 5 yards (4.6m) ⅜-inch/9mm-wide red satin ribbon
- White sewing thread
- White felt
- Sawtooth hanger
- Decorative-edge scissors (optional)
- Needles: #16 tapestry, sewing needle
- Hot-glue gun

Stitching Step by Step

Basket

Referring to General Instructions, page 2, cut basket front and back from plastic canvas; stitch in pattern using white yarn. Back with white felt. Sew sawtooth hanger to reverse side of basket handle at center top.

Poinsettias & Ornaments

1 Cut six small and six large poinsettia petals, four small and seven large leaves, and six ornament shapes according to graphs.

2 Stitch poinsettia petals and leaves according to graphs, working Straight Stitch at tip of petal or leaf last, and Overcasting edges with matching color.

3 Stitch ornaments A–D and Overcast edges according to graphs. Stitch and Overcast one ornament E according to graph; stitch second ornament E substituting Christmas red yarn for green metallic craft cord.

Assembly

1 Using decorative-edge scissors if desired, cut a ⅝-inch (1.6cm) and a ¾-inch (1.9cm) circle from yellow craft foam for poinsettia centers.

2 Referring to photo throughout, arrange poinsettias on basket front, using one small leaf, five large leaves, and large petals for poinsettia on left side, and remaining leaves and petals for poinsettia on right side. Glue yellow foam circles over centers of poinsettias.

3 Onto a doubled length of white thread, string seven gold beads; knot thread ends tight to form a ring of beads. Glue beads to foam center of larger poinsettia. Repeat with remaining beads; glue to foam center of smaller poinsettia.

4 Cut a 3-inch (7.6cm) piece of gold metallic craft cord. Knot ends of together, leaving a 1-inch (2.5cm) loop. Glue ends to reverse side of ornament at center top edge. Repeat to add hanging loops to remaining ornaments.

5 Tuck ornaments into basket; secure with glue.

6 Cut ribbon into three equal pieces. Fold each in half and loop around top of basket handle, allowing streamers to dangle behind basket and hang 15–16 inches (38.1cm–40.6cm) below bottom edge of basket. Trim ribbon ends at an angle.

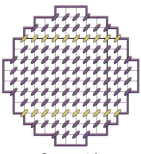
Ornament A
13 holes x 13 holes
Cut 1

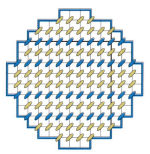
Ornament B
13 holes x 13 holes
Cut 1

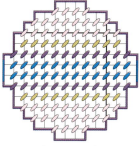
Ornament C
13 holes x 13 holes
Cut 1

Large Poinsettia Petal
7 holes x 15 holes
Cut 6

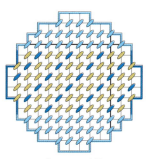
Ornament D
13 holes x 13 holes
Cut 1

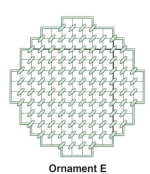
Ornament E
13 holes x 13 holes
Cut 2
Stitch 1 as shown, stitch 1 substituting
Christmas red for green metallic

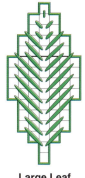
Large Leaf
7 holes x 15 holes
Cut 7

Small Leaf
5 holes x 12 holes
Cut 4

Small Poinsettia Petal
5 holes x 10 holes
Cut 6

COLOR KEY	
Yards	**Plastic Canvas Yarn**
14 (12.8m)	■ Christmas red #02
11 (10.1m)	■ Holly #27
92 (84.1m)	■ White #41
1 (0.9m)	■ Bright blue #60
3 (2.7m)	■ Bright purple #64
	╱ Holly #27 Straight Stitch
	╱ Christmas red #02 Straight Stitch
Craft Cord	
5 (4.6m)	■ Gold metallic
3 (2.7m)	■ Green metallic
2 (1.8m)	■ Multicolored
Color numbers given are for Uniek Needloft plastic canvas yarn.	

Copyright © 2007 DRG, 306 East Parr Road, Berne, IN 46711. All rights reserved. This publication may not be reproduced in part or in whole without written permission from the publisher.

The full line of The Needlecraft Shop products is carried by Annie's Attic catalog.
TOLL-FREE ORDER LINE
or to request a free catalog
(800) 582-6643
Customer Service
(800) 449-0440
Fax (800) 882-6643
Visit AnniesAttic.com

We have made every effort to ensure the accuracy and completeness of these instructions. We cannot, however, be responsible for human error, typographical mistakes or variations in individual work. This publication may not be reproduced in part or in whole without written permission from the publisher.

ISBN: 978-1-57367-269-6

Printed in USA

1 2 3 4 5 6 7 8 9

Shopping for Supplies

For supplies, first shop your local craft and needlework stores. Some supplies may be found in fabric, hardware and discount stores. If you are unable to find the supplies you need, please call Annie's Attic at (800) 259-4000 to request a free catalog that sells plastic canvas supplies.

Before You Cut

Buy one brand of canvas for each entire project, as brands can differ slightly in the distance between bars. Count holes carefully from the graph before you cut, using the bolder lines that show each 10 holes. These 10-mesh lines begin in the lower left corner of each graph to make counting easier. Mark canvas before cutting, then remove all marks completely before stitching. If the piece is cut in a rectangular or square shape and is either not worked, or worked with only one color and one type of stitch, we do not include the graph in the pattern. Instead, we give the cutting and stitching instructions in the general instructions or with the individual project instructions.

Covering the Canvas

Bring needle up from back of work, leaving a short length of yarn on back of canvas; work over short length to secure. To end a thread, weave needle and thread through the wrong side of your last few stitches; clip. Follow the numbers on the small graphs beside each stitch illustration; bring your needle up from the back of the work on odd numbers and down through the front of the work on even numbers. Work embroidery stitches last, after the canvas has been completely covered by the needlepoint stitches.

Basic Stitches

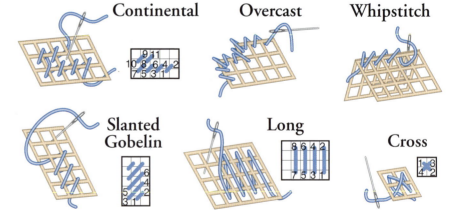

Embroidery Stitches

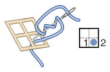
French Knot

Lazy Daisy

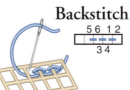
Backstitch

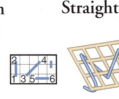
Straight

METRIC KEY:
millimeters = (mm)
centimeters = (cm)
meters = (m)
grams = (g)